# Earth Angels

Thea Clark

# *Dedication*

I dedicate this
book of poems
to my soulmate

Shawn Ren Owens

Thank you
for allowing me
to borrow your
wings until mine
were ready to

open      again

## *Wings*

Those words escaped that mouth
and crept down my throat
Planting seeds in the pit of my belly
They grew inside of me
Pulsing through the heart
Wrapping around veins
Blooming out of these shoulder blades

## Creator

I am a creator
I come from above
I breathe the wind
I birth the dove
I touch the stars
I speak with trees
I light the fire
I am free

## *Star Fire*

I am
haunted
enchanted
undone
by the sound
of that voice
spread across
time
kindled within
my soul

# Love

The walls society constructs
will not contain me
The box fear built
will not shame me
The matrix projected
will not sustain me
The hate that festers
will not drain me
The truth that burns
will deeply stain me
The joy that spreads
will forever frame me
The peace that whispers
will proclaim me
The love we carry
will ordain thee

## Crooked

Crooked lies
Crooked smile
Crooked life
Crooked mile

*Seeker*

If you seek out love
it will be found
If you seek out evil
it will be found

## Intimacy

Lick these lips
Taste this tongue
Ignite our fire
Swallow desire
Smell the sweat
Feel our pulse
Ride this wave
Bodies cave

## *Disappear*

Kiss me

Tempt me

Grab me

Leave me

## Asral

We meet

in dreams

the space

between

eyes closed

mouth open

eyes awake

daybreaks

## Madness

Are you brave
enough to swim
in the depths
of your desire
or will you
drown in seas
of fear
when I light
your holy fire

# Goddess

Aphrodite

Whispers in my ear

Dances on my tongue

Moves through my hips

Sings your siren song

Drinks the wine

Ties the cords

Drifts away

Unadorned

## Merlin Grins

White horse

Silver armor

Soft hands

Heart of honor

Warm kiss

Slow lover

Torn apart

Her king's brother

## Beware

You linger there
Unaware
Strip me bare
Without a care

## *Tower*

Born to be
misunderstood
Destined to fall
Where will you be
When I sound the call

*Co-Creation*

I am not yours
You are not mine
We are the Universe
Intertwined

*Light*

The brightest of stars
have tasted
the darkest of depths

## Moonlight

She woke from her sleep,
as streaks of moonlight
poured through the window.
The air was light, her soul, aware.
Energy danced around the room.
Teasingly, as if to sweep her
into another
realm.

*Spirit Guide*

Green eyes seduced my soul
White hair caressed my cheeks
Pink lips painted kisses across my chest
Soft skin traced symbols down my body
Alluring voice praised my name
Bright smile lit my life

## Empress

I am divine
Abundance seeps
through my skin
Flowers sprout
from my spine
The world orbits
in my belly
Hands sift
the sands of time

## Mother

Mother of creation
She rose from the dust
Fire breathing maiden
Creature born of lust

## Judgement

Unweave the webs
that grew from pain
Wash in waves
of desire untamed
Worship the beauty
designed in your heart
Don't let earthly
judgement tear you apart

*Levitate*

Lock the door
Lift the sheets
Lick the love

*Downstream*

I
find
inspiration
between
these
thighs
poetry
pours
out
of
you

# We

Who am I
Who are we
We are one
Eternally

## Fear

Wish me well
Let me go
Cast your spell
Resist your flow
Break my heart
Shed your tears
A life apart
Led by fear

## Halos

Lift your head

Open arms

Let love loose

Angelic charms

Feel fear flee

Sacred souls

We will wander

Life unfolds

## Human

The sun kisses my lips
The moon pulls my hair
The ocean bathes my body
The earth strips me bare

*Escape*

Run with me
Don't look back
Let's lose time
Trace love's track

*Appreciation*

Let us forget our worries
Bask in the sun
Worship each others bodies
Completely come undone

## *Siren*

Lady of the lake
Grant me a wish
Will you come now
Succumb to a kiss

## Guinevere

Heavenly beauty
Rosy cheeks
Flaming hair
Man's defeat
Loved by two
Bound to one
Set her free
Let her run

## Mary

Pure heart
Loving soul
Holy portal
Took its toll

## Cleopatra

Raw power pumped
through her veins
Sweat dripped like
gold from her skin
Women offered
their hearts at her altar
Men worshipped
the ground she graced
Emerald snake slithered
up her spine
She conquered all
even the divine

## Persephone

She spoke softly in my ear
Made my worries disappear
Planted flowers in my heart
Shot me with her lover's dart

## *Live*

We never truly wanted to die
We wanted to dance disastrously
We wanted to live beyond measure
We wanted to love passionately
We wanted to create constellations
We wanted to feel freedom
We always truly wanted to live

## Threads

Our hearts aligned
By heavenly design

## Baptized

Felt nails sink into skin
Burning fire from within
Bit their lip
Licked the blood
What saints call
A sacred flood

## Fortune

Jupiter covered her in kisses
Dressed her in flowers
Confessed eternal love
Blessed her potent powers

## Whispers

The winds blew
then I knew
this lonely heart
belonged to you

## *Tulip*

I pluck
thoughts
from my
mind
like petals
and wonder
if they are

yours

or

mine

## Fire Signs

Our love is all
encompassing
Burning eternal
at the core
Flames
twist together
binding
our unforsaken lore

## Shine

Let us vanquish
these fears together
Watch them crumble
at our feet
Our love will
light the planet
No need
to be discreet

## Monarch

I will never be conquered
I will never bow
I will never cease to love
I will always wear this crown

*Self*

What will you find
when thoughts of others
leave your mind

## Torture

Do you feel me
in between your thoughts
See me in your dreams
Escape was never an option
Surrender the only release

*Source Energy Being*

They felt our souls
coming
When our feet hit
Earth
Shattering illusions
Echoing truth
This will be our
birth

## Keeper

Keeper of

souls

Charmer of

hearts

Sweep us

away

Tear us

apart

## *Bloom*

May I always speak softness
into the world.
If any words of fear ever cross my lips,
know that they are an illusion;
for the only truth that exists is my love.
I believe that certain events are
predetermined.
That our souls expand eternally
from the contrast.
Even the darkness
we plant in one another is a gift.
A seed that will transform us into
something beautiful.

*Divine*

Red wine
Cross the line
Moon trine
Forever mine

## Emperor

I love you
in ways which
mere mortals
could never fathom
My lord
I surrender
For you keep
my blooming chasm

*Eclipse*

Enter divinity
Enchant humanity
Escape reality
Embrace eternity

## Release

Rain drops
Heart stops
Sky cries
Love dies

*Coming Home*

There was something
familiar about the way
your hand fit in mine
Destined to find one
another across all
space and time
How your mouth curved
the first time we kissed
A reunion of souls
your hair in my fist

# Body

I love my big beautiful ears,
for they were passed down from my Grandpa.
I love the stretch marks that appeared,
as I grew into the woman I am now.
I love the dark circles under my eyes,
a manifestation of all the thoughts I have ever pondered.
I love the scars that grace this skin,
a reminder to slow down and embrace each moment from within.
I love living this human experience.
I love this flesh and these bones.
I love this body as it transforms.
It is my home.
It is my cathedral.
It is my vessel.
It is my altar.

*End*

She floated
like an angel
waiting to be devoured
What a lovely ending
this bright burning tower

## A note from the author

For all the hopeful romantics out there.
Keep on loving. Keep on shining.
Keep on believing.
I hold steady to the belief that we are all one.
That our souls come from
Source energy, and when the time comes;
we make our way back.
There is comfort in knowing that love is the
core of our being, even when we find ourselves
pinched off from it.
We may be capable of
anger, sadness, and hatred.
However, it is not truly who we are.
I encourage you to look within for the love
that you seek, and watch for evidence of the
love that you are,
as it begins to pour into your reality.
You are worthy, you are powerful,
and you are loved.
Always.

## Acknowledgements

Mara Lilith,

the purest heart I have ever known.

Angel Holyfield,

the strongest spirit to grace my life.

Elle,

the hope you carry inspires me eternally.

Andre,

your passion for life keeps the fires lit.

Asher,

the wisdom within will set you free.

My tulips,

thank you for showing me how to love

unconditionally.

## About the author

Thea Clark
graduated from Central High School in Peoria, Illinois,
where she studied drama and dance.
She later became a certified
energy worker and author.
Her breakthrough as an actor came
when she played the cigarette smoking woman in
the Lionsgate picture Pursuit (2022).
After appearing in a number of television series
including The First Lady and Doom Patrol,
she was cast in the holiday television special
A Waltons Thanksgiving.
In which she portrayed Mrs. Windham.

Pacific Publications

P.O. Box 441 Norfolk Island NSW 2899

Copyright © 2023 Thea Clark

Internal design @ SIDUS LLC

Cover design & Artwork © SIDUS LLC. All rights reserved. The characters and events portrayed in this book are a product of the author's imagination or are used fictitiously. Any similarity to real persons, living or dead, business establishments, events, or locales is coincidental and not intended by the author.

No part of this book may be reproduced, or stored in a retrieval system, or transmitted in any form or by any means, electronic, mechanical, photocopying, recording, or otherwise, without express written permission of the publisher, except in the case of brief quotations embodied in critical articles or reviews. Any brand or product names used in this book are trademarks of their respective holders and are not associated with Pacific Publications. Printed in the United States of America

ISBN: 978-1-922936-44-8

www.ingramcontent.com/pod-product-compliance
Lightning Source LLC
Chambersburg PA
CBHW070338120526
44590CB00017B/2931